JOSHUA CAPRAI

the coyote soul of a janitor's son

poems by joshua caprai

Copyright © 2020 by Joshua Caprai

All rights reserved. No part of this publication may be reproduced, stored or transmitted in any form or by any means, electronic, mechanical, photocopying, recording, scanning, or otherwise without written permission from the publisher. It is illegal to copy this book, post it to a website, or distribute it by any other means without permission.

First edition

This book was professionally typeset on Reedsy.
Find out more at reedsy.com

Foreword

to all of the people
   that i have ever
   written about

to all of you that
   have taken up
   residence in my heart
   and to all of you
   that have since
   vacated

to all of the folks
   that i speak to
   everyday
   and to those i've
   only seen in passing

to all of you that
   i love
   and hate

and to those i've
   not yet decided
   which i feel for you

i dedicate this to you

to the bums i shared
   a bus station with
   in the dry valley heat
   of california

to the one i meant to marry
   and to the many distances
   that inevitably grew between
   our hearts

to the blood brother
   that remained
   who once danced with opiates
   on the full moon
   and to the dance
   he now dances
   with his son

to the little brook
   that never stopped
   trickling
   and grew into a mighty
   river

to the stone throwers
   and the monoliths
   we created and
   hurled away

to the old gargoyle
   with a heart of gold
   who helped me
   find the sea

to mrs. robinson
   and to the sympathetic eyes
   that can no longer
   look upon you
   to the bridge
   and to the water

these are
   for you

as much as
   they are
   for me

i thank you for everything
   and apologize for

nothing.

painful airwaves

the radio is relentlessly playing broken hearted songs
   while my father
   fresh out of a divorce
   looks on

he's thinking hard
   feeling hard
   and driving hard
   you could always tell
   when he was doing the first two
   as he would be doing the third
   every time

his mother passed on
   only weeks ago
   and so
   no shoulder to cry on

nobody understands your pain
   like your mother does
   and now
   with nobody to understand

THE COYOTE SOUL OF A JANITOR'S SON

    his broken heart
    he weeps

he weeps at the low
    aching feeling in his gut

that terrible tingling
    sensation that rattles
    his bones

he mourns in the most painful
    way i have ever seen a man mourn

torment
    gnashing of teeth
    wailing
    howling at the moon

and all i could do was watch
    and try to understand
    but there's no
    understanding
    that pain

because his mother is gone

and nobody understands your pain
    like your mother does

and so he looks on
    and the radio is relentlessly playing broken hearted songs.

fool's gold

california is perceived as
   some sort of fantasy
   resort
   where you forget all
   your troubles
   and soak up
   the beautiful sun and
   beautiful weather

and beautiful people

truth be told
   california is just a place
   where you go
   in hopes
   that the rest of the world
   will forget you

and a place where you can
   get good mexican food
   and just disappear

but it still gets dark sometimes
   in sunny california

california is a painted pony
   chipping and warped
   stuffed behind boxes of polaroids
   in a desert shed

california is a tiffany bracelet
   behind the wrought iron
   barred
   windows of a pawn shop

california is a high school yearbook
   water-logged from
   the flood
   "see you next year" written
   in the back

california is a beautiful girl
   on heroin

california is a lot of things.

death in fall

willful
   solitary
   confinement of the mind

black out the lights
   lock the doors

nothing gets in
   nothing gets out

board up the house

keep it to yourself
   burden no one
   but yourself

pending deconstruction
   renovation
   renewal
   rebirth

we can only hope

it will work this time.

horses

walking on the
   cracked sidewalk
   down e street
   in encinitas
   looking at my feet

trying not to
   step on the
   cracks

my back has already
   been broken
   a few too many times

a gust of wind blows
   and there is an
   overwhelming scent of
   listerine

i look up
   and away from my feet
   and there he stands

THE COYOTE SOUL OF A JANITOR'S SON

a thin
   gangly man
   with large scabs
   covering most of
   his visible
   extremities

hair, far beyond
   sun bleached

leathery skin
   and a vest to match it
   the man's name
   is terry
   and he does not
   have a home

he asks me for
   some spare change
   i give him the 11 cents
   from my pocket
   which he is
   unenthusiastically
   grateful for

i ask him for
   a cigarette
   and he rolls me
   a bugler-on-bugler

he starts up

HORSES

    about the del mar race track
    and his secret to winning

13-to-1... you've got 5 horses, right? that's 1, 2, 3, 4, 5. now one those horses is 13-to-1, guaranteed to win, okay? so you just-and here's the trick here josh-you look at the program from the last race, find any scrapped tickets that are on the ground or in the trash because sometimes people throw away their tickets before the end of the race and that's my ticket right there.. and find your 13-to-1. its that simple, josh. that simple.

i reply simple with
    a few nods and
    ah i see
    or
    oh okay yeah
    that clearly meant
i had no fucking clue
    what he meant

he was too sauced
    to have noticed
    so we bullshitted some more
    and he talked about the races
    and i interjected my
    simple responses

until about an hour
    had passed
    just shooting the shit
    with terry, the local bum

he asked me for the time
   and i told him a quarter to ten

shit, i've gotta hoof it back to del mar, races end in two days, gotta make it, gotta find that winner that 13-to-1 hey josh man you oughta come out there sometime before the races end in two days we can make some serious money oh hey got any more spare change so i can get a beer it's a long walk to del mar man

i gave him five dollars
   i could've used it
   but he needed it
   more than i did

he thanked me
   this time very enthusiastically
   and grateful
   he packed up his
   various items
   and with a leathery handshake
   off to the races

i later found out
   that he went to jail
   on a murder rap

i picked up my
   various belongings
   and started down
   the cracked sidewalk again

HORSES

   looking at my feet
   trying not to step on the cracks

a gust of wind blows
   and there's an overwhelming
   scent of cheap brandy

and there stands another
   thin gangly man
   made of leather and
   totally gone

hey brother, can you spare some change for a beer

and off to the races again.

el segundo blue butterfly preserve

a new one
   a brand new bag
   of butterflies

you know
   the bug
   but not the
   breed

look at all the colors
   blood reds and
   flame oranges and
   deadly blues and
   toxic greens and
   grim blacks

aren't they a wonder

prepare your net
   bide your time

the thrill of a chase

EL SEGUNDO BLUE BUTTERFLY PRESERVE

   you'd long forgot the
   feeling

your plasma pulses
   desire
   want

it has been years
   your net
   torn
   you take your shot
   swing lo
   and mighty

you are not alone
   for many admire
   the colors

it has been years
   you are old
   slow

frailty comes for you

you miss

blood flushes from you

too late

the colors captive now

take up your net
   blow your trumpets

go home

the thrill was worth it this time
   wasn't it?

martyr

some will say
   they never
   saw it coming

others
   who knew
   will say

i didn't think he would
   but i knew that
   he thought a lot
   about it

they will write
   these things
   in the yellowed
   pages of the news

they will say
   these things
   through tears
   at the service

it will be a surprise
   to most
   if not all

there will be few
   who attend
   fewer that
   truly knew me

many will make statements
   but not
   at the service

sometimes the statement
   itself
   suffices enough

i can see it now
   who will be there
   their faces
   veiled and solemn
   are one of the few
   reasons i talk myself
   out of it

believe me
   when i say

i do not refrain
   for my own sake

MARTYR

i refrain
   for the veiled
   solemn
   faces
   in attendance

i love you all
   too damned
   much.

salud

such
   a naysayer

nothing
   nice to say
   about anyone
   ever

i sip my beer
   as she lays it on me
   say nothing

just a sad
   sad man
   who wants
   to bring everyone down
   all of the time

go ahead
   take your
   misery out on the rest
   of the world

SALUD

it will do you
   no good

sip

you're no good
   and you want
   everyone to know
   feel bad
   and buy you
   beer

my ears prick up
   at that last word

sure
   i'll have another round

on you

damn it
   she says
   and calls to the bartender

another sculpin
   on my tab please

thanks

i sip the head
   off the glass

wipe my mustache
  start in

you know
  honey
  you're right

i'm going down
  always been
  headed that way

don't have any
  plans to get back
  up again

tried once
  or twice
  maybe a few more

only direction
  i've known is
  down

i'll be damned
  to hell
  if i let you
  or anyone
  sit there
  and make me feel bad
  about taking them all
  down

SALUD

   with me

not without
   buying me a fucking beer
   first

the good ones
   die young
   so they say

the bad ones
   die slow
   alone
   sink
   to the very bottom

as brass rusts
   the band's tune
   keeps on
   fading
   out

we bad ones
   looking
   for company
   on the way
   down

and someone to buy
   the next round.

that old vineyard

sometimes i enjoy finding old lovers
   just to see what
   they've been doing
   who they're with now
   how their lives are

but mostly to see if
   they've gotten more
   attractive
   since we were together
   and if i have a
   chance
   at getting them back

most of the time
   it's the former and
   not the latter

some people age better than others

some grapes become fine wine
   some get eaten by the bugs.

modern dentistry

some days you smile
   at people and
   they don't smile back
   sometimes
   it ruins your day.

some days you
   smile at people
   and they smile
   back and sometimes
   it still ruins your day.

cupboard

to all of the women
   who only ever called
   when their man dumped them
   on the side of the road
   at 2 o'clock in the morning

or got drunk and
   beat the hell out of them

to all of the women
   who told me they loved me
   when their fiancés were deployed

to all of the women
   who referred to me as
   their guilty pleasure
   dirty secret
   and kept me hidden away
   in the dusty cobwebbed compartments
   in their heads and hearts

to all of those women

CUPBOARD

    and to their men
    thanks
    for making me feel

somewhat useful.

abattoir

the dog is growing tumors everywhere
   plants are turning brown

she says
   you smell bad
   more than she says i love you

i have more
   scars than tattoos
   now

the house sags and bends
   paint peels off

dog won't stop biting
   a hole in her leg

destroying herself

never fully awake anymore
   stop breathing in
   my sleep

ABATTOIR

drink more coffee
   than ever

drink less beer
   than ever

quit smoking
   eating red meat

trying to fight it
   reverse it

but there is a difference
   between aging
   and rotting.

national geographic

short sharp bones
   grow out of fingers
   short sharp bones
   grow out of gums

for tearing
   slicing
   shredding
   built to kill

born this way
   created to destroy
   bred for this

i watch animals
   tear each other
   and wonder

what sort of god
   could make such
   horrible beasts

NATIONAL GEOGRAPHIC

what sort of
  person would give
  offering
  to such a god

paying him
  to make more
  beasts
  mindless
  machines of mortality

then
  i'm reminded
  the very same
  people
  though smarter
  more upright
  would do the
  same
  things
  to each other
  if their money was
  all gone

driven to primal instinct
  they'd tear at the
  flesh
  of their neighbors
  of their bosses

all because the money is

gone

   it is really something
      how the difference between
      animals
      is measured
      only

   by green pieces of paper
      and little silver coins.

010312

two days
   into a new year
   a fresh start
   and i fucked it up

my future is
   on hold now because i
   departed
   lost it
   and beat the hell
   out of my assistant manager

i resolved
   to start anew
   and i guess
   that's what i'll do

every new year
   should be christened
   with the blood
   of an authority figure.

fire watch

tried to live
   the country life

settle down into
   a quiet green
   holler

but there is
   still
   smog in my
   eyes

still asphalt in my palms

when you've sprouted
   from a small
   unknown world

there is no romance

to the sleepiness

FIRE WATCH

the quiet is
   too quiet

the vast emptiness
   fills you up

you are both containing
   and contained

in the void

the great void never sleeps, seth.

there will be refreshments

funerals are the best time

to make the dead
   seem brighter
   than they had been

everything the living ever
   bitched about
   the week before
   never happened

everyone's a
   liar at the
   altar

truth would be
   far
   far
   too much for
   the mourning to bear

they are the real victims

THERE WILL BE REFRESHMENTS

    aren't they

do you think they have
    funerals
    because it pleases the dead

hell, no

the dead are
    dancing
    with the
    dead

as the folks in black
    pay respects to
    their own
    loss

when i am gone
    don't grieve

fuck ceremony
    and service and

do not

put my corpse in a
    church

when i am dead
    just have a drink

THE COYOTE SOUL OF A JANITOR'S SON

it's on me
   this time

then get on
   with your damn lives

quit moping already.

searchers

it does nothing
   good for you

makes you
   sick and
   crazy

should you be worried
   always

should you even ask
   absolutely not

do you really want to play that game
   never again

spend your alone time
   playing it out
   in your head

every detail
   clear

it's happened before
   you were right
   before

you let it go
   didn't you

ask yourself
   if that was wise

your best interest
   becomes
     least concern

can't say
   you enjoy it

but the addiction is there

no rest for the sickened
   no eye in the storm

weiss said
   the cure for the pain
   is in the pain

you've rolled that
   around for years
     trying to make sense
     of it

SEARCHERS

maybe the cure is in the words
   somewhere

but the words fire out
   of you
   an aimless arrow

look for somewhere to
   stick
   get caught in a gust
   and fly off

if the cure for the pain
   is in the pain
   or in the words

the search
   does nothing
   good for you.

brooks hatlen

there were chains that
   held me down

bars that
   kept me in

walls that
   closed in on me

one day
   i was set
   free

the door swung open
   chains came undone
   walls fell down

i was
   free

now that i'm free
   i'm lost

BROOKS HATLEN

familiarity gone
   the world too big
   i'm afraid
   of this
   big open
   space

now that i'm not
   in love
   i'm more lost than ever.

stuck

on good days
   you're the
   toughest motherfucker
   to walk the block

untouchable

on bad days
   you're lucky to be
   the gum stuck to the shoe
   of the toughest motherfucker
   walking the block

still untouchable

think about that
   next time you

take a walk.

this is a gift

if you had cared
   if you weren't selfish
   you would have
   given us a better life

if you loved us
   if you wanted to see us
   flourish
   you would have
   put us in a good school

if you weren't
   preoccupied with
   your own wants
   disguised as
   gods will
   you wouldn't have let us
   go hungry

if you were not
   full of pride
   you would have

taken better jobs

you trusted your god
   would provide

you believed gods word
   would save us

you told us
   it was god calling you
   to move us all over

did god provide
   did he protect
   did he watch over

what good did your
   god
   do

there never was
   any word or will
   of god

it was your own
   disguised as
   holy manifest destiny

god is man's justification
   for his own selfish
   desires

THIS IS A GIFT

god is not dead
   because god was never there

neither were you.

#44

early
   always too early
   awake all night
   howling mad drunk
   wailing
   cursing
   at the moon till
   runs away

and the innocent shine
   morning brings
   those god damn early birds
   singing their god damn early songs

over the creaking old
   cars that struggle to
   get going
   coughing up their late night
   drives into the atmosphere
   and shuffle and sputter towards
   the great
   big

junkyard

sad
   poor
   aching mothers
   walking innocent
   shining children to
   innocent shining school

too early
   always too early
   or too late

the world
   dreary
   dark
   cloudy
   rainy
   sinking
   while i sink further into
   the old mattress on the floor
   of upstairs apartment #44

where it's always too early
   or always too late.

twitching

i keep it
  locked up

this rare bird
  for me
    to look at

here
  for my admiration

feathers fall out
  plucked out too

but i cage
  so well

would rather
  fly and sing

maybe

could it enjoy

TWITCHING

   this

imprisonment

there are no
   locks
   not really
   anyhow

and it is a
   smart creature

adaptable and
   cunning

it could
   might
   escape

oh my

it could

but i chain it
   with words
   and money
   things
   sex sometimes
   shelter
   comfort
   stability

THE COYOTE SOUL OF A JANITOR'S SON

i see it in
   the eyes

the nature
   the will to roam
   free

a wilderness caught
   in somber and
   hazel eyes
   but

you know

i could never stand
   being alone.

note to self

you have
  every reason
  to worry

about the awkward
  pimpled kid
  you went to school with

the one who always wore
  sweatpants to school
  no matter the weather

who always had his books
  and his binders
  and pencils with him

who had a small
  circle of
  equally pimpled
  awkward
  friends

you have
   every reason
   to worry

about the kid who
   was once
   your only friend
   when you were the
   new kid in town
   who was bad at
   math

the kid who
   ate lunch with you
   when all the
   cool kids
   laughed at you
   because multiplication
   was not your forte

the kid who
   told you about his
   grandmother's ferret
   as if it were the
   funniest thing
   on planet earth

you have
   every reason
   to hate yourself
   for turning on this kid

NOTE TO SELF

for making new friends
   and finding a table
   to sit at

for making fun of him
   to make your new friends
   laugh

for treating him
   like you were never friends
   at all
   like he never did
   a thing for you

you have
   every reason
   to worry
   about him

and you have
   every goddamn reason
   to hate yourself for it.

like anthony

i can't stop it

the quick snap
   the sudden drop

pulling tight

the kicking
   convulsing

the throttled breaths

i hear them
   all day

every day
   obsessively

reminding me of how
   quick and painless

it could be

LIKE ANTHONY

refreshing relieving release

my spine pulled taut
   chin to the stucco

looking for what ever images
   you found there in your youth

could be anything now

you stopped seeing things
   like that years ago

now it's all dead things in the corner
   voices from the bathroom

avert your eyes kid

look up and away
   one more time

see for yourself
   there was never anything there

but man,
   a kid can dream.

liturgy

the goddamn
   morning hours

why am i awake
   what do normal people
   do during these
   early
   treacherous
   times

i find
   i have an increased
   sensitivity to
   light
   though i'm
   uneasy in the dark

been laying here
   too long
   my back hurts
   more than one place

LITURGY

interesting how
   even our bodies
   get bored with the
   same old
   shit

interesting how
   the number twenty-three
   is an enigma
   so they say

interesting how
   in rainforests
   men
   women
   and children
   die in the heat
   to make
   girl scout cookies

but i still can't
   get any sleep
   in these goddamn morning hours.

silverware

those of us
   with difficult lives
   those of us
   struggling
   those of us
   poor

we grow
   mighty
   contempt for
   anyone we
   see with more
   money
   less struggle
   more happiness
   and the like

we proclaim
   gee, i sure wish I didn't have
   to work for anything
   i wish i was born into an
   easy life

SILVERWARE

    fuck those bourgeoisie yuppies
    and their nice new clothes

we blame our misfortune
    on our lot in life
    and sneer
    at young men
    in pressed three-piece suits
    and slick haircuts

they've got it
    so
    damn
    easy

a future served
    with a silver spoon

while we slave away
    and eat our
    canned meals

with plastic utensils

the truth of it?

yuppies and
    socialites
    have tremendous
    luck
    make all the

    right decisions
    that lead
    to their comfy
    velvety
    upstairs loft

that is their
    silver dinner set

good
    goddamn
    luck

my father used
    to say
    there's no such thing as luck
    only faith
    and god's plan

i think most
    men
    with terrible luck
    say this
    often.

hangover poem

when the whiskey's gone
   and the cigarettes
   burned out

and you're going down

when the birds start singing
   and so do you

that early morning
   purgatory
   between drunk and hungover

heaven and hell

where we find ourselves.

life sentence

believe me
   when i say
   i have every intention of
   committing suicide

not
   soon
   more than likely once i'm
   old and
   in the way

once i've done all
   i planned to do in my
   lifetime
   at least enough
   to say i had a good
   long
   run

such punctuation gives
   a life more
   dignity and

LIFE SENTENCE

    profoundness

as a sentence
    changed entirely
    by the placement of punctuation

especially when it's
    your own ink
    that presses that
    final character into
    the paper

you wouldn't want
    someone
    or something else
    finishing that sentence for you

would you?

ornithology

all i can do
   anymore is
   get mad
   at my sadness

the sadness that
   comes out
   when i'm alone at home
   a cave with my thoughts
   some nocturnal blackbird
   in my chest

perhaps that means
   daylight happiness
   isn't so real
   just a temporary
   painkiller
   that makes me forget
   about the little blackbird
   singing away

maybe that's just

ORNITHOLOGY

   the duality of life

there is no universal
   happiness

without the melancholy
   in the dark
   happiness is incomplete

maybe the morning birds
   can't sing their songs
   without the blackbird

and all i can
   do anymore
   is get mad

that damned bird is keeping me up all night.

the winds

scrambling now
   hurried and rushed

the thrill ain't gone but
   you're gonna need to
   do some throttling
   to find it

red faces and
   gasps

handprints showing you
   how to fight for air

the fight is all you got now

gazing up at the
   stucco

you remember the wind chimes
   at the polio lady's place
   across from dad's church

THE WINDS

first time you heard someone say
   pervert

imagine the sound the
   wind'd make
   if you crushed them

a wolf's whistle
   a kink in a windpipe

what's the difference
   between a pipe and a
   chime anyhow

new veins on your
   forehead

right before you
   let go
   slump down

the fight is all you live for now

polio lady is probably dead
   now
   that was then

the thrill ain't gone
   but you'll have to
   choke the life out of it

to find it again.

jesus piece

this is
   one of the days
   i want to
   hide

don't have the energy
   to face it

want to give in
   to the world
   then destroy it with
   my fists
   brick by brick

run away to empty spaces
   scream in a
   vacuum

to a god that i
   wish were there
   so i could give him a piece of my mind

THE COYOTE SOUL OF A JANITOR'S SON

for some peace of mind

this one of the days
   i should have slept through.

braces

this smile is
  a stress fracture

grin and bare it all.

hunting accident

close your eyes and dream
   of the places you
   used to be

go home
   see for yourself
   they aren't there
   you're someone else

the house isn't there anymore
   there's a strip mall now

carl is retired now
   your dad doesn't drive the honda
   mom is married in the desert

the walmart you lifted condoms from
   remodeled
   the mall you lived in
   cole isn't there now
   his hair is short now
   he has a child and

HUNTING ACCIDENT

   his leg isn't broken anymore

your hair is short now
   styled
   you can't ride on the front of the scooter

you can't call stevie
   stay at his house above the pharmacy
   with scott's sister

those albums are 10 years old now

she's married now

nobody likes those bands now

you can't go home
   you can't go back

this gun is a time machine
   say hi for me.

modern mechanics

i used to daydream
   think all day
   out the back seat window
   of a ford sable

dad said it was champagne colored
   i said it was dirt colored

still haven't had champagne
   that color

i used to daydream
   about faking my own
   death

to make my older cousins friends
   sorry
   for making fun of me
   calling me a freak

little did i know
   they wouldn't have

MODERN MECHANICS

    cared at all

little indeed
    could i know
    how many
    deaths

i would die

just when you thought
    it couldn't possibly
    be worse than this

i used to daydream
    out the back window
    of a ford winstar

mom said it was dirt colored
    it's a good color for the mojave

i imagined spike strips
    and oil slick
    coming out the back

warding off tailgaters
    and assholes in PT cruisers

how many do you count seth

i dunno, i think it was seventeen in needles

THE COYOTE SOUL OF A JANITOR'S SON

i used to daydream
   out the back window
   of a geo metro

everyone agreed
   it was eggshell white

i imagined stealing my
   grandparents'
   dolphin motorhome
   me my cousin and my brother

and taking it to san diego

that was mecca then

a paradise away from this
   endless bomb testing
   sonic boom
   rocket site
   desert town

i was sure kaleb could drive by then

little did i know
   what homelessness
   was like

what it would feel like

to be drunk

MODERN MECHANICS

on new years
alone
on a filthy vinyl kitchen floor
30 millers deep
wrists flayed wide

calling home

wishing i could be
  in the back seat of a
  winstar
  sable
  or geo metro

little indeed
  could i have known

one day i'd be daydreaming
  again
  for a home
  to come back to

i used to daydream

but there's no time
  not now.

the future

we met 11 days ago

days are years
   now
   too fast for me

we were kids
   11 days ago

i was thin back then
   you called me river

older now than
   he was
   that night outside
   the viper

i wrote volumes
   for you
   destroyed most of them

lost in the fire

THE FUTURE

felony arson

its criminal
   the way our innocence
   burned

i don't know how
   to slow it
   down

get me back
   to the terminal

this ticket was
   given to me

i will not take
   the ride

jane stop this crazy thing.

daily routine

one of
  these
  days

i will
  make
  someone
  as happy
  as they
  make
  me

one of
  these
  nights
  i will
  sleep
  peacefully

without
  interruption
  from pains

DAILY ROUTINE

   both
   physical
   and
   well..

one of
   these
   mornings

the sun
   will
   shine
   as brightly upon
   me
   as it
   does upon the innocent
   things
   of the earth

and i will arise
   and
   conquer

a new day will come
   by god
   it had better come

one
   of
   these
   days.

constructive

it was right after
   the election
   that i told him

came along with a rant about the
   state of things
   new president and all

he said he loved me
   no matter
   like it'd change how

i know he feels

we'll talk more about it soon
   he said

that was the last
   mention of it

he's good at pretending
   my father

CONSTRUCTIVE

makes short work of
   boarding it up
   painting over

he always was good with his hands

i know it
   crushed him

oh god
   his eldest son

he'd failed somewhere
   raising me

don't think there's a
   book on his
   shelf for
   this

it happened to his brother
   now me

what is this world coming to
   men behaving this way
   nobody is born with it
   blame the media

ah, well
   i don't want to talk about it with him
   either

THE COYOTE SOUL OF A JANITOR'S SON

i learned that
   much from
   him

how to be good with my hands
   to mix plaster
   to patch it up
   sand down
   paint over

like nothing
   even
   happened

now we can both
   pretend

i'm straight.

which one's pink?

the goddamn vultures
   won't let him be

there they lay
   your hero

gone
   not before their time
   but too soon
   for you

ain't it always
   too soon

when they still breathed
   nothing could touch them
   couldn't falter
   and they never gave in

everyone wanted a piece

hey we want you in our commercial

THE COYOTE SOUL OF A JANITOR'S SON

    let us use you
    we want to brand you
    you'll make millions
    and did we tell you the name of the game, boy?

they were bulletproof to all of it

now they're gone

wings crack thru the air
   here come the bastards

keen
   to pick bones
   clean

all your shouts
   stones thrown
   bounce off
   the mighty crooked beasts

we're just here
   to pay our respects
   see

they speak thru bloody beaks

the carcass now raped
   of what it held in life

winged thieves fly into trees

WHICH ONE'S PINK?

carrion in tow

you'll hear a jingle soon
   on your television
   a faint moan you
   almost recognize

it's your hero
   only distorted
   somehow

vapid and dried

their image is now
   quaint and
   kitschy

everyone just wants to pay their respects

the goddamn vultures
   won't let him go.

the romantic type

she left
   blonde hairs
   on the mattress

that blanket she
   made for me
   smells like
   her

that smell is
   more beautiful than

any poem
   any song
   any bird
   any sunset
   any flower
   any dress
   any painting
   any angel
   any angel
   any angel

THE ROMANTIC TYPE

more beautiful than
   any angel

just one night
   she slept
   i slept
   in the same room

i let her have the
   mattress

i don't mind
   the floor

waited
   my whole life
   to be there

couldn't help
   but think

she deserves
   so much more
   than i have
   to give

heart sinks
   further down
   but
   nothing

THE COYOTE SOUL OF A JANITOR'S SON

not my heart
   not the trees
   not the poems
   not the sea
   not the words
   not even the rain

matters now

there are
   angel hairs
   on my mattress.

tracking

a fool
   waiting and waiting
   cutting for sign

looking for smoke

won't make the
   first move this time

you tell it to the mountains

set up camp
   ask the stars
   they do not know shit

walking the ground over

fuck it

brandish your call
   hear its echo

THE COYOTE SOUL OF A JANITOR'S SON

emptiness
  void

you knew before you even came here

the errand of an idiot
  heartworn
  grade-A
  dumb ass

the sky never
  answers your
  cries

but cry you will

a lonesome
  bull-headed
  coyote

who's lost his sense
  of smell

scent washed away
  by record rainfall

gone now
  fool
        you have always been bad at this.

junkies and preachers

there will always be
   suicidal people

people who cannot grasp
   the concept
   the absolutism
   the finality
   of death

who don't understand that
   you don't float
   above your body
   when you die

and get to see
   all the people mourning
   your death

once you're gone
   you
   are
   so

THE COYOTE SOUL OF A JANITOR'S SON

    gone

and no deal with any deity
   will bring you back

there will also
   always be the people
   who do grasp

the concept
   the absolutism
   the finality
   of death

who will remind you
   of how precious
   your time
   on earth is

but goddamn, aren't they a buzzkill?

the rains

streets
  shimmering
  black
  asphalt boiling
  over the
  sidewalk

my head and hat
  drenched
  as i walk
  to pacific station
  in a December
  downpour

shoes splashing
  plodding along
  the long walk
  to the station

every step
  like bone
  grinding

THE COYOTE SOUL OF A JANITOR'S SON

   against
   bone

rusty cogs
   in an old
   worn machine

spine
   knotted
   and twisted
   round

like wrought iron
   fences
   of cemeteries

twenty one
   years
   out the factory
   and already
   experiencing

difficulties

the warrantee
   long
   void
   by faulty
   titanium upgrades
   and inspections

THE RAINS

can't
  return it
  for a new one

already been
  twenty one
  years

a shoe slips
  and hands
  flare out to
  catch the falling
  body

but the hands, too
  slip
  scrape

the face
  kisses ground
  no dry spot
  to be
  found

splash

i lay
  soaking
  cursing
  aching

to hell with work
   to hell with pacific station
   and to hell with california

stood
   twist
   crack
   pop
   continue
   onward

can't afford to
   miss
   another day
   of work

these are
   the rains
   you've read
   about.

little bear

there i am again
   swept away
   into cobweb corner

amongst the chipped china

waiting
   my turn

stay there they say
   i'll be back for you

cupboard slams
   light shuts out
   eyes adjust
   cough
   dust unsettled

brought up from the
   last time

you let thyself be

THE COYOTE SOUL OF A JANITOR'S SON

   thrown back into place
   where you belong

   thanks again
     for making me feel
     useful.

meat hangar

it's funny
  the way you
   love to watch
   me beg

you coax it out
  i see the look
  you wait
                so you can shame me for it

i see that lust
  in your eyes

you lie on your couch and wait for it

a hunter in his blind

nothing gets you off
  anymore.

he's gone soft on us

the softest
   thing

every
   part
   of you
   silken and velvet

my rough and scarred
   hands ran over
   all of it

you would just
   lay back
   kiss me
   gently

let me
   explore

a beat up
   mangy dog in awe

HE'S GONE SOFT ON US

    of the softest thing
    it ever saw

i thought i would
   hurt you
   with these calloused paws

but no
   i would come to hurt you

without ever using my hands

ashamed of my damned sentiment
   ashamed of my damned shame

you slipped through the cracks
   in my palms

nothing feels
   soft
   anymore.

#92

this is the most domestic
   I've ever felt

there are more spiders
   in this complex

than there are dogs

coincidence?

rambler

was it something
   that i said

in those
   early days

i said a lot then

that made you
   think i was
   ready

to slow my hand
   settle down

been known to
   say a lot
   i do not mean

if you thought
   you had a ticket to

    stability
            you must've folded some corners

we warned each other
   do you remember

you said you could be so cruel

i said i'd never stop my rambling
   we both said that's okay

we both lied

you used to like me
   for my writing
   told me when i
   visited
   you'd force me to write

embraced it

now you tell me
   i never had it

you're a fake
   you told me

you don't write about anything at all

so i hid it
   away from you

RAMBLER

in notebooks
   stuffed into bags
   in the typewriter
   i haven't used since you got here

it's all there
                      waiting to see the light
                      one day i'll show them
   i'll show everyone
   what you made me hide

i don't do too much talking
   these days.

improvement

chicago had a historic
   sweep today

i am laying on the
   floor with my
   head on a damp towel

pretending to fix a
   leak under the sink that
   does not exist

jansen looks back
   to form

and kershaw

my glasses are fogged
   or greasy
   or both

i should never be allowed

IMPROVEMENT

    to wear white
    she said
        the miracle mets might make it again this year

the dog is smelling my
  dirty foot

she puts on a southern
  accent when
    someone from texas calls

do not try to be a hero again rios

i see the leak now.

apnea

ah
   now you remember

that thousand yard feeling
   the stove might as well
   be in another
   room

the crawl never been so long

at least the floor is
   cleaner now

taken care of
   spoiled again

you always find
   your way

act like prey
   but you know what you are

APNEA

goddamn fool

i'd have called you
   pathetic
   6 years back

now you're in the bathroom before work
   thinking about someone
   that ain't thought of you for
   years

they have kids now

don't you get it
   you don't get to play
   with people like
   you used to

you'll never grow up
   will you?

another bullshit poem written to validate it
   like an audience can read it
   like anyone cares

no one cares but
   you

you
   and whomever you've been writing to
   all these years

THE COYOTE SOUL OF A JANITOR'S SON

now you remember

there was never really anyone
  you were never really
  there
  neither were they

wake up, kiddo
  you're late.

the greeks

some call their lover
   a muse

they
   inspire them
   to be a better
   person

a guardian angel keeps them
   in line

i can't come up with a good reason to think so
   highly of someone else

museless
   uninspired
   unguarded
   out of line

i don't hold
   anyone
   up that high

yet
  i am
  growing jealous of

the mused
  the inspired
  the guarded
  ones

being alone
  it isn't all
  bad

just lonely

sometimes lonely makes you
  crazy

sometimes crazy
  jumps

off bridges
  off buildings
  out windows
  onto sidewalks

yeah

sometimes
  jumpers don't jump

THE GREEKS

sometimes crazy sits
   home
   alone
   lost
   scared
   uninspired
   museless
   useless

but i'm not crazy
   are you

punch and judy

this will be
   that straw

you know the one

fourth job
   in three months
   that didn't work out

got fired
   not enough hours
   not enough pay
   place closed before it opened

where has the
   luck gone
   indeed

sitting on the loading dock
   waiting for the news
   presumably
   bad

PUNCH AND JUDY

aaron pulled up
   twenty minutes ago
   told me we might not
   have jobs

he's in there now
   talking to them

and i'm waiting
   like a cat
   in a box
   possibly alive
   possibly dead

suspended
   my usual state
   in this life

it can't
   just be me

nobody
   is this much
   a fuck up

right?

it's got to be
   the luck
   or lack thereof

she's gonna leave me
   if i lose this one

i know it

we yell every day

kiss and make up

but the yelling gets worse
   every day

and always about the jobs

it's always my fault
   i'm too lazy
   unmotivated

that might be
   partially true

but i didn't make this place close

listen to me

talking like it's already
   happened

i'm still waiting

guts knotted up

PUNCH AND JUDY

   like the strings
     of an old puppet

suspended
   my usual state

in this life.

lesser solomon

the devil
  put those thoughts
  into your head

he says

those are not
  your own, son

you mean
  the devil
  makes me think
  things?

how do i keep
  him
  out?

he makes me
  want to
  kill
  that boy that

LESSER SOLOMON

   beat me?

he makes me
   think about
   the dead
   knocking at my window?

does he make me
   see the
   dark figure
   in the corner?

you are made
   perfectly
   in god's own image
   he says

huh
   i guess
   it would make
   sense

that god
   would be so
   tortured
   at the mercy of thoughts
   not his own

but thoughts
   planted there
   by the devil

    himself

god is not
  omnipotent
  if he is powerless in this
  earthly
  realm
  is he?

i am a reflection
  of a god
  marred by
  time
  and earth

holding up
  in fear and faith
  a facade
  of strength
  power
  control

in front of
  a withered creature
  in chains
  bound to satan
  himself

there is no eternal struggle
  the devil is man
  man is the devil

LESSER SOLOMON

god is an
   afterthought of a constructed
   conscience

an excuse for
   bad behavior

i am the son of man
   here to reconcile
   my own nature

i am a product
   of the world
   denying the existence of
   my basic instinct

i am god
   i am the devil

i am a goddamn
   son of a
     bitch.

racing

it's funny how
   inconsistent
   fear is to me

how
   in one situation
   that would scare the absolute shit
   out of a grown man
   make him weep like a child

i felt nothing

not a tear
   nor a chuckle
   just
   fucking
   nothing

or in another
   instance
   that any
   normal human

RACING

    would find no real fear or anxiety in

i shake like a leaf

terrified
   gutless
   tears welling up

seemingly without
   any goddamn reason

stomach in
   infinite knots
   thousand-yard stares
   into the abyss of
   a wall
   or tree
   or anything, really

the first time
   i went to jail
   i laughed the whole
   car ride there
   laughed in the holding cell
   laughed during the pat-down
   laughed in the waiting room
   laughed in the dress-in
   laughed in my no-mattress bunk
   laughed when my cellmate stuck a broken pencil in his throat
   laughed during lockdown
   laughed at breakfast

    laughed in the dress-out
    laughed when i got out

the last time
    i went to meet a girl
    at her hotel room
    i stood in front of the door for what felt like
    an hour

shaking in front of the door
    shaking when she hugged me
    shaking when i uncorked the wine
    shaking when she kissed me
    shaking when we fucked
    shaking when i slept
    shaking when i got my clothes on and
    shaking when i left

even now
    as i write this
    my hands are shaking

my guts are on fire
    my head is a horse race

maybe i need to go back to jail

might be able to hold still
    long enough to write a
    goddamn poem.

a free man

he stands
   hunched over
   eyes closed
   playing card held
   behind his back
   says

come on baby, gimme a winner gimme a winner

slowly
   his hand pulls forward
   eyes closed
   card faced away
   he opens his eyes
   one at a time
   and flips the card around

yes! yes! yes! who's your daddy, eh?

his long
   green
   sun bleached hair

THE COYOTE SOUL OF A JANITOR'S SON

   tied in a bun
   with feathers stuck in it

he dances a circle
   switching from one foot
   to the other

card in hand
   tallboy Steel Reserve
   in the other

i stand
   no more than seven feet
   from him
   and watch
   chuckling

he has no idea
   i'm there
   no idea
   he's there

there
   under a dim streetlight
   the alley behind
   the art gallery
   the wayward native son
   the homeless hometown hero
   the last of the mohican warriors of 1st street

isn't much difference

A FREE MAN

    to him
    between the cell
    he left
    on good behavior

and the worn out cafe table
   in the alley behind the
   art gallery

then he sees me
   calls me jason
   as he always has

happy holidays
   he says year-round

say you don't got a spare dollar or two for beer do ya just a
beer ya know just a little beer
   i say i'm broke

he shrugs
   picks a piece of popcorn
   from the ground
   pops it in his mouth
   chugs the rest
   of his reserve
   and promptly crushes the can
   puts it in a plastic
   grocery bag

we don't have conversations

much anymore
i'm too busy
running by
and he's more a drunk
now
than when he went inside

say bro you got a locker in your work can ya stash somethin
for me it's real important and i gotta give it to cheryl at the
library tomorrow man it'd really help me out just til tomorrow
ya know

he furnishes a blank
   cd from his bag
   says terry 11/24 on it

it's real fuckin important man i need to keep it somewhere but
I can't give it to jagger ya know he's a fuckin shithead he'd just
piss on it or hell i dunno anyways can ya stash it for me jason
it'd be a big fuckin help

i say yes
   put it in my bag
   not entirely sure
   what's on it
   and entirely sure
   i don't want to know

say thanks a lot man they oughta give you a promotion in there
bro you're a hell of a young guy and when you're the big boss
man you can get me free coffee right heheheh

A FREE MAN

so long
  i say
  and
  happy holidays

i leave for the job
  carrying potential
  incriminating evidence

and the knowledge
  that i'll never have
  a dull moment
  as long as that
  crazy
  wild
  drunken hawkeye
  is out of jail.

the seer

i look at a person
   and imagine
   how they'll look when they're old
   washed up
   leather-skinned
   dead inside

what kind of shit job
   they'll be holding
   how many kids
   they'll have
   how poorly
   they'll raise them

the spouses they hate
   because they married
   out of wedlock
   not of love or courtship

the piece of shit car
   they drive to work
   every morning

THE SEER

the dilapidated house
   on it's sinking foundation
   they live in

the empty beer cans
   the ashtrays of cigarette butts
   the old television on some local news station
   the torn leather couch
   the kitchen crawling with pests
   the dishes in the sink
   the fridge full of beer
   and not food

the high school diploma on the wall
   with it's broken promise

all i see is the future in everyone
   all i see and hear is shit.

drainage

the hill going down
   rancho del oro drive
   is steep

the air smells
   of salt water
   and local flowers
   that smell like cat piss

the old mission
   illuminated
   at the bottom of the hill

part of me
   wants to break in
   and confess it all

taking walks at three in the morning
   has become
   a routine
   on the nights i'm off work

DRAINAGE

i'm either drunk
   lonely
   or a hellish combination
   of the two

i'm in hell
   as i write this down

the night has been
   my favorite time
   for awhile now

though i was
   deathly afraid of it
   as a child

no people
   few cars
   cold air

the way the street lights
   glow and reflect
   deep orange
   off of the wet cement

the streets on fire

best time to
   clear your head
   sober up

THE COYOTE SOUL OF A JANITOR'S SON

all i hear
   are the patter of my shoes
   on the concrete
   traffic roaring
   like lions
   far away

and my mind is full
   of things
   i wish i could empty
   onto the asphalt
   into the sewer

out to sea

but this old dome piece
   doesn't have
   a release valve

and all things
   build up
   steam in a pressure cooker

waiting to blow

occasionally
   seeping out
   through the mouth
   nearly unintelligible

folks get a glimpse

DRAINAGE

    of the things they don't
    understand
    and don't care to
    understand

and i suppose

i can understand why.

black dog

thought about it today

what i'd do
   if you walked out
   on me

left me alone
   again

surely i would
   try to drown in
   bulleits and key strokes

throw something dramatic
   and wordy
   together

wouldn't even
   want to go out
   get fucked

that would make it

BLACK DOG

worse

i've written this
   five hundred different
   ways

about five hundred
   former lovers

how i just
   wouldn't be able
   to go on living
   without

i convince myself
   that each new one
   is the only one
   I've felt this way
   for

that the storms
   will be record-breaking
   this year

i should stay inside
   pull up the mattress

it's going to get
   nasty out there

it is always worse

    inside the house
    though

I worry myself
   sick
   as
   a
   dog

left at home

it feels like
   years gone by
   every time
   you leave.

joe dimaggio and graveyard shifts

i've sat here
   trying
   hard
   to write something

that would
   do some
   justice
   in your next
   life

which you found
   the door to
   at the
   bottom

of the

jump

from coronado bridge

i can't
  find any
  words

that would be
  fair

to write
  about someone
  who's
  passed
  isn't
  easy

one shouldn't write
  selfishly
  or quickly

i write nothing
  i deem worthy

except that i'm sorry

i hope
  the answers you looked for in
  this
  life
  are in the
  next

here's to you, mrs. robinson.

sidewinder

you don't know
   and you never
  will

the things i've let my
   mind do

a measure of control i
   willingly
    let go of

i live subdued from
   the rest

in constant fear of
   spilling it

maybe you've caught
   a passing glance

i drink too much and

the grip
slips
briefly
momentarily
but enough
to make you raise an eyebrow and wonder
if you imagined it
not me

gaslight you
   play it off
   change the subject
   laugh at you
   pay my tab
   return home
   crawl back to my hole
   slither away
   coil up close
   and remain

i'll make myself
   sick
   with the things i let my mind do

if they only knew, god
   they'd put me away for good.

freaks

the t.v. shows a
   program about a
   freak show

says
   normal is relative

that they are
   just a normal family
   full of dwarves
   giants
   sword swallowers
   tattooed women
   fire breathers
   horribly disfigured people

they cook like a
   normal family
   but they don't look
   like a normal
   family

the t.v. insists that
   normal is relative

the same t.v. that
   shows commercials full of what
   normal should look like

normal clothing
   normal families
   normal smiles
   normal hair
   normal bodies
   normal cars
   normal skin
   normal people
   that cannot relate to anyone
   at all

i think that the t.v. is a hypocrite.

bela lugosi

you are
   a husk
   a shell
   abandoned

there is nothing
   inside you
   but blood
   guts
   piss
   vinegar

soon there will be nothing.

leadbelly

i have died
   1,000 deaths

little ones
   mostly

a door slams
   lock clicks
   dog shivers in the corner

and there is a death

fuck you
   you're a loser
   i want to go home
   do you think i deserve this

another death

a tossed book
   hand grips wrist
   and shakes

LEADBELLY

   bruises

death

how many times
  can one die
    before the end

infinitely

there is no end
  to the death

every day

the smoke clears
  but leaves it's tarred
  brown stain

stomach aches
  like it used to

burning
  warm

it is a fire
  in the belly

means that
  the end
   has not come

yet

coals
  sparks
  fire
  smoke
  ashes
  dust

that is life

burn out or
  fade away

depends on how long
  you can withstand
  the heat

death and fire
  will keep me alive
  through another
  endless
  night

and i'll be just fine
  sleeping on the couch
  again.

1:36 a.m.

the barking dogs
   far off
   in the distance
   sound like an angry
   drunken
   passionate
   and emotional argument

and vice versa.

spoilage

they won't leave
  me
  be

the flies
  they smell the
  death

coming

i'm toast
  fucked
  ruined
  doomed

i worry and worry

dying is hard

but i'll come alive
  again

SPOILAGE

in another state
   another career
   another lover

for now

the flies smell the death.

john waters

pink flamingos
  two of them
  in our yard

bought them
  together
  set them so that
  their necks
  made a heart

cute
  couple
  shit

lovebirds
  first place together

aww

month has gone
  by

one of the birds
   started leaning
   crooked like

the cheap
   paint
   on their beaks
   rubbed off
   already

metal legs
   rusted

lease is up
   in five months

they won't last that long.

sundowning

getting there

the point
  where
  can't ever seem
  to sleep enough

wake up
  can't find my way
  around the house
  for at least
  an hour

can hardly
  walk

pain is too
  much
  these days

the machine
  is giving

SUNDOWNING

   up

can hardly
   recognize
   friends anymore

all look like
   cardboard
   cut-outs of
   people i saw
   in a mall somewhere

possibly
   Oklahoma City
   maybe Lancaster
   could be
   Springfield

the malls all
   look the
   same now
   too

i get lost
   too easily
   these days

walk in
   circles

frustrated

THE COYOTE SOUL OF A JANITOR'S SON

    confused

you are here
    says the directory

everyone else
    they are

far
    far
    away

and my vision
    gets worse
    with each night
    i lie awake
    through

a scratch
    across the
    lens.

over time

gonna take
   a quick ten, tom

hold down the
   fort

out the kitchen door
   down the hallway
   up the stairs
   into the stall

this could be
   it

might be
   the day

ceiling is
   high enough

belt strong

THE COYOTE SOUL OF A JANITOR'S SON

secluded

wouldn't find
  me
  at least a half hour

that'd be
  it

fort would go on
  being held down

poor tom

he'd have to
  work overtime

because of me

more money for him

i'm selfless
  like that

could be
  the night

but it isn't

not tonight

OVER TIME

lavarse las manos
   salpicar la cara
   mirar en el espejo
   volver al trabajo

un y otra vez
   y otra vez

and again.

family matters

i don't
  think the importance
  of having
  family
  around all the time
  applies to all
  families
  across the board

see
  i'm a naturally
  negative person

this issue is
  rooted in my
  family tree

i do my best
  of course
  to remain positive
  and find simple
  joys in life

FAMILY MATTERS

but when i'm near
   family
   for any length of time
   i am drained

never have a
   decent thing
   to say
   about any
   damn thing

always saying

i'm just feelin' sorry for myself today

or

why don't you ever call me? what about my feelings?

it's always about
   them

only about
   them

but god forbid
   you ever
   say anything
   to them
   about it

they're family
   after all
      right?

with relatives like these

who needs a guillotine?

cashing in

going crazy
   cracking up
    losing it

the girl at the register
   doesn't smile at me
   like she used to

she made eyes at me
    when we were introduced
    seemed interested

i swear she did

just like that
   no more eye contact
   no extended conversation

the words coming
   from my mouth
   don't make sense

THE COYOTE SOUL OF A JANITOR'S SON

i imagine them leaving my mouth and
   turning to visible
   characters

nonsense
   words strung together
   without rhyme or reason

while she looks on
   as though i've spoken
   a foreign language

requisite
   hushed
   hurried
   response
   no conversation

just replies
   affirmations
   fewer
   less frequent smiles

people in line
   ahead
   she talks to them
   about school internships
   and futures
   smiles
   laughs
   conversation

CASHING IN

while i babble
   about wine
   and the civil war
   in some language
   foreign to her

and i think
   i'm going crazy
   cracking up

i must be losing it
   i gather my change
   and receipt and
   move along.

classified

seeking

psychological torture
   expertise

passive aggressive
   tendencies

emotional distress

at least
   two kinds of
   mental disorders

extreme
   sexual deviancy

and a powerful
   lust

for the cinematic arts.

don ciccio

i have the weakness again

for the likes of people
   that have the
   nice watches

but can't give me
   the time of day

i know where
   i belong

gun molls
   barkeeps
   bad ass bitches

grab you by the
   crotch and scream

get off your ass
   bum

THE COYOTE SOUL OF A JANITOR'S SON

enough feeling sorry

go earn your bread

but i dream sometimes

of my own two
   dirt ridden hands

tearing up clay
   somewhere north of morocco
   building my house
   hand hewn brick
   by hand hewn brick

it is a beautiful house

years pass in my slumber
   in its construction

and then i wake up

and then i earn my bread.

omaha

i asked her not
   to hurt me
   like begging a tiger
   to keep it's claws
   sheathed

i told her i would
   abide her woes
   like telling a child
   daddy is just
   going away for a while

i tried to hide the
   wound
   like asking a shark
   not to smell the blood
   in the water

nothing violates this nature.

manners

women in the west
  do not like to
  be called
  ma'am

because it
  reminds
  them of their mortality

women in the
  south like
  to be
  called ma'am

because it reminds
  them of their
  mortality.

coagulate

lost a lot
   of blood

accident
   or by my hand

doesn't matter

it's gone now
   isn't it

new blood pumps
   replacing the old

but for a moment
   before the pump

that lost blood
   sits
   in a puddle on the ground
   or a smear on the wall

THE COYOTE SOUL OF A JANITOR'S SON

you watch it
   oxidize
   dry
   crackle
   fade

get your shit together
   patch yourself up
   spill more blood
   maybe someone else's

and then you move on
   and forget the blood
   you've lost

then you bleed again

katmandu

people travel
   from all over
   the place
   to look at things

folks without a coast
   come to the coast
   to stare at the
   roaring ocean

to be inspired
   by its
   might and beauty

i stand at the
   edge of a bluff
   hoping it will
   make the words roar
   out of me

people from the coast
   go to the midwest

to see depression and heat
and cold
and to feel
cultured
i guess

people from the west
   go to the east
   to see how rude
   the people are there
   and to see the
   fall colors

so on
   so forth
   they go forth

to places they haven't seen

they go to see
   and experience

and then
   some folks
   just hate traveling

they like to stay put
   wherever they are
   maybe out of content
   maybe out of fear

KATMANDU

i am certain
   i do not know

one thing
   i am most certain of however

is that you catch
   a lot less flack
   from people in the midwest
   for smoking cigarettes

maybe they're hoping
   that you'll start a fire
   and make something
   interesting
   happen

and i stand here
   at the edge of a bluff
   drag and puff
   thinking real hard about the ocean
   on fire

shangri-la aflame

burning one
   in
     paradise

now there is something i would travel
   to see.